D1219770

What It Means to Raise a Child

WITH

Southern Manners

A Reflective Perspective
From a Girl Raised Southern

~

by Cecilia Budd Grimes

What It Means to Raise a Child

WITH

Southern Manners

Copyright ©2005
by Abram & vanWyck Publishers

For additional information on youth silverware,
as referenced in Chapter 9, call the
What It Means To Be Southern toll-free number
877.968.2555 for patterns, pricing, and shipping details.

All rights reserved.
No part of this book may be reproduced
or transmitted in any form or by any means,
electronic or mechanical, including photocopying, recording,
or by any information storage and retrieval system,
without permission in writing from the publisher.

Published by
Abram & vanWyck Publishers
North Carolina
www.WhatItMeansToBeSouthern.com

Manufactured in U.S.A.
Design by Paula Chance, Atlanta, GA

Library of Congress Cataloging-in-Publication Data has been applied for.
ISBN 0-9708396-3-4
First Edition

"Train up a child in the way he should go,

and when he is old,

he will not depart from it."

Proverbs 22:6

TABLE OF CONTENTS

~

So do we raise our children or rear them?

My Webster's New World Dictionary tells me that to rear a child is *"to bring to maturity by educating, nourishing . . . to put right, to elevate."* That hits the mark and certainly, by most anyone's standard, is a significant and crucial undertaking, and Southerners, and not just Southerners, take this noble enterprise seriously. But Southerners rarely refer to the process of bringing up their children with the more technically correct verb form. Just like their references to "uptown" and "downtown," they mean the same thing to a

1

Southerner. Serious grammarians aside, Southerners declare the process as one of raising.

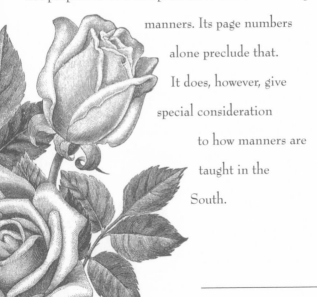

This book is a primer, and as such, does not cover all the topics or situations that could emerge under the large umbrella term, manners. It certainly does not purport to be a comprehensive text on teaching manners. Its page numbers alone preclude that. It does, however, give special consideration to how manners are taught in the South.

SOUTHERNERS commonly use the designation *"Y'all"* which is a contraction for *"You all."* Its use is widespread throughout the South and used widely in both oral and written form. (Note the apostrophe always follows the Y.)

3

References to Scripture are from the *Holy Bible, King James Version*

Dictionary definitions are taken from *Webster's New World Dictionary of the American Language*

" Just a reflection
of my raisin' ..."

Precious, lovely, and darlin'

HOW WOULD YOU DEFINE A CHILD as one raised with Southern manners? I'm not sure, even after writing several books, if I were up to such a task, but I certainly do know one when I see one and hear one. And so do neighbors, grandparents, family members, and friends from work and at church.

Generally speaking, children raised with Southern manners would project kindness and consideration as manifest in such behavior as:

- Conveying proper consideration for others by including *"Excuse me"* or *"Pardon me"* when a lapse in proper decorum has occurred, saying *"Thank you"* as an indicator of gratitude, offering *"Please"* when making a request, and responding with *"You're welcome"* to complete a gracious exchange

- Signaling respect for elders by such gestures as using an honorific with a surname and relinquishing a seat to an elder

- Offering a proper handshake with eye contact when being introduced

- Refraining from profanity, vulgarities, or any pronouncement that could be considered sassy

- Maintaining an appropriate sense of decorum in public places

Children should be taught to stand when guests enter their home. (Yes, that means teaching them to interrupt watching the DVD or playing Monopoly® and greeting the guest with *"Hello."*) Those who have lived many years have earned the courtesy of being acknowledged by standing. In doing so, our children learn to honor longevity and esteem their elders.

- Extending appreciation and goodwill by writing notes

- Showing visible affection to people we value and esteem

- Exhibiting proper eating skills wherever the setting

What a tall order! Just remember it evolves over a lifetime of learning, but the sooner the process is begun the greater the measure of benefits to family, friends, and self! Look at it as the gift of another gracious soul to the universe.

"Manners certainly count

BUT

Etiquette Matters!"

Things Dear to Our Hearts

EVERYONE HAS MANNERS of one sort or another, and people are never hesitant to describe how another person's behavior, whether an adult's or a child's, comes across to them. That's why we hear such a wide range of descriptions: *"She has such lovely manners." "His manners were atrocious." "What rude children!" "Her granddaughter's manners touched my heart."* And on and on.

The Senior Forum* recently featured a list of pet peeves from those living in their golden years.

Imagine my dismay to read that Peeve Number 8 was *"undisciplined and impolite grandchildren"* listed alongside other concerns like taxes, and Social Security, and estate planning.

That should not be, and so this book is an attempt to address some of the issues that confront

Retirees list peeves of golden years by Kent Collins, Sunday, August 8, 2004, News & Record, page 5D

and confound us as parents of precious, lovely, and darlin' children who inevitably will act up, misbehave, and cause consternation, often deep and abiding, for their parents. I believe children have minds of their own and will misbehave—even when they've been taught better. We just must keep diligently to the task of teaching them right from wrong over their formative years.

There are two keys to that discipline. First, the correction should be immediate, "nipping it in the bud," correcting it right when it happens, not later—even if that requires taking the child aside at times otherwise inconvenient for the parents. Manners cannot be taught on delay. The other key is consistency, which requires teaching the same principles, the same expectations without exception day in and day out. It has been said growing old is not for the faint of heart. Neither is child raising!

Etiquette addresses these very issues because etiquette is a knowledge base and can be learned, just like computer skills or a new language. Etiquette defines for us whose name should be said first (the more important/higher ranking person) in a correct introduction. That knowledge tells us that when we introduce a new friend to our grandmother, we

Boys *and* girls should be taught to shake hands. A correct handshake connects each hand firmly at the web between the index finger and the thumb. The Protocol School of Washington® calls this grip "web to web." No more pinched fingers when the grip is correct!

should say our grandmother's name first because she is older and deserves our respect. *"Grandmother, this is my friend, Alaina, who is on my swim team."* (In the grown-up world, if your parents meet the Mayor of the town or a Judge from court, the elected official's name would be said first.)

In European countries, young children are taught to shake hands, but we are more informal in our introductions. Eye contact is important, as is a smile, and a proper handshake is icing on the cake!

"Bless your heart!"

*Your mama and daddy would
be so proud . . . "*

IT'S BEEN SAID that common courtesy is not so common anymore. That's a shame because Mama and Daddy always stressed the importance of Southern courtesies, and making your Mama and Daddy proud of your Southern manners, even after they've gone on to their reward, remains a very big thing.

Rate your "common" courtesy, Level I.

Use yesterday as the day to rate a Southern child:

☐ Saying *"please"* when making a request

☐ Thanking verbally someone who has done a favor for you

☐ Using a kind and pleasant, rather than demanding or sarcastic, tone of voice

☐ Walking to the right in a hallway or a lobby

☐ Avoiding interrupting anyone who is speaking

Teach your young child to put his or her hand on your forearm, without speaking, when he or she wishes to speak. This silent gesture signals a request to speak, without interrupting the conversation. Parents should commend the kind manners of the child when permission to speak is granted.

15

- [ ] Allowing a person senior to yourself to enter into a doorway, elevator, or escalator before you

- [ ] Stepping aside immediately after you exit an elevator, escalator, or a doorway so others coming behind you aren't blocked

- [ ] Holding a door open for others, especially those who are older or physically challenged

- [ ] Waiting to begin eating until others are served in your immediate group

- [ ] Apologizing when you call a wrong telephone number

☐ Resisting the urge to "break in line," even when encouraged by friends

☐ Identifying yourself by name when greeting others and when placing a telephone call followed by a request

_____ out of 12

Scoring 12 out of 12: Excellent beginning!

Scoring less than 12, keep reading!

Rate your "common" courtesy, Level II:

Once again, use yesterday as your day to rate.

☐ Offering a handshake, web to web, as an appropriate response in a formal introduction or as a gracious greeting and looking the person in the eye with a smile

☐ Standing up when an accomplished person/guest of honor/person of rank or importance enters the room

☐ Introducing yourself to those at your table or those seated immediately around you at a gathering

☐ Waiting for permission to eat (or a signal from the hostess) before beginning

☐ Introducing classmates or friends unknown to each other

☐ Calling people by name during greetings

☐ Writing a thank you note for any gift

☐ Responding in a timely way to an R.s.v.p.

☐ Resisting the opportunity to rush from the back of a checkout line ahead of others to go to a newly created line

☐ Placing your cloth napkin into the seat of your chair when you leave the table as a signal to the wait staff you will be returning

☐ Offering food first to the person on your right
at a table setting before serving yourself

☐ Pacing your eating to match those dining with
you so you're not the first to finish nor the last

☐ Moving through a buffet line with purpose, so
as not to hold others back

☐ Resisting the urge to load a plate of food to
over-brimming, to gather handfuls of complimentary candies or favors, to overindulge on
"freebies" when access is unrestricted

☐ Foregoing an opportunity to respond harshly
or with sarcasm

☐ Taking advantage of any opportunity to do
something kind, even if it's a small gesture

A score of 16 out of 16 denotes *Outstanding
Courtesy!* Scoring 16 or less, keep reading!

"Yes, Ma'am"

A N D

"No, Sir"

is music to our Southern ears . . .

SOUTHERNERS CERTAINLY DON'T HAVE A LOCK (as the old expression goes) on good manners, but I think it is fair to say that Southerners have special expectations of what good manners involve. And to Southerners that includes saying *"Yes, Ma'am"* and *"No, Sir"* religiously and without apology. Using *"Ma'am"* and *"Sir"* is a courtesy taught across Southern generations and is a defining element in raising children with Southern manners.

It's pretty basic to Southern manners, and learning to respond to our elders with *"Yes, Ma'am"* or *"No, Sir"* should be taught at a very young age. Many people from other parts of the country either discourage this Southern courtesy or are dismayed by it.

Ma'am explanation
A polite title used to refer to a lady . . . a shortened version of madam

Neither matters to born-and-bred Southerners who value these pronouncements as both proper and important indicators of courtesy and respect. You'll be hard pressed to find a Southerner raised Southern who could be talked out of using these respectful responses. Our mamas and daddies spoke it before us, as their parents did before them, so it's an entrenched custom that is valued and practiced. Even two-year-old Southern babes, just beginning to talk, are taught to follow this tradition—and without apology.

Saying *"thank you"* and *"please"* are likewise important.

When correcting a child who tends to bypass this standard courtesy, a parent will often prompt a child with *"What did you forget to say?"* or *"What's the magic word?"* to which the child will usually respond *"Please"* or *"Thank you."* To reinforce an automatic response that includes such niceties as *"thank you"* and *"please,"* it's better to train the child to restate the *entire* request including the *"please"* as part of another whole sentence, rather than allowing the child to respond with the one single word that is being solicited. A child should be taught to repeat the entire request again, incorporating the courteous word, so it becomes second nature. This approach reinforces the inclusion of courteous words as part of any request of others or any acknowledgment of a kindness.

"Goodness gracious,
I'd love to come . . .

but only if I'm invited."

THE PROBLEM WITH INVITATIONS, from a manners point of view, is that they are often misunderstood and frequently misused, if not abused. People show up at occasions to which they are uninvited. Often uninvited children are brought along for convenience sake. Sometimes people neglect to reply, leaving the host or hostess open to a guessing game of who will come and who won't. (How large a room should I reserve? How many people will be served food?) Many times people respond affirmatively to an invitation and then don't show. Other times they respond with regrets and then appear. Etiquette precludes all such inconsiderate responses. We should teach our children better.

   Here's a way to know who's invited: the name appears on the invitation! Weddings are a good place to start. Wedding invitations that include double envelopes list the primary guests on the outside envelope, sealed and with a stamp, and include others, including children or guests, on the unsealed inside envelope. Sometimes the phrase "& Family" is included, which gives wide acceptance to all guests within the family.

Brides and their parents are conscientious about the wedding list, and a guest has a guest duty to abide by the wishes of their hosts.

Remember the rule of etiquette: a host or hostess, by virtue of being host, has the privilege and right to determine the type of occasion, the site, the number of guests to invite, and other such considerations as menu items, entertainment, floral arrangements, and the like. The rationale is simple: the host is paying.

Guest duties are to appreciate the opportunity to attend, respond—affirmatively or negatively

—to the invitation by the date and manner listed, and show up with good manners, if a decision is made to attend.

What we should not do is bring along uninvited guests, including our children.

Over the decades I have encountered more than a few guests who felt slighted that their children were not invited to occasions to which they felt entitled to bring them. Their expressed indignation included a refusal to attend themselves. This reaction is a misunderstanding of host privilege and guest duties and is unfortunate because on many occasions hosts are not seeking to offend but simply prefer an adult gathering.

We love our children, but not one of us has been exempt from witnessing a young child who is restless from being restricted to a church pew or a restaurant chair. And it causes consternation for others,

especially when the occasion is
quite special such as an anni-
versary or wedding celebration.
De-sensitize yourself to a per-
ceived slight, if your children are
not invited to adult occasions.

27

Our manners reflect how we value others, and
we need to remind ourselves that such a thing as
host privilege does indeed exist, and that it outranks
the wishes and inclinations of those invited. No
grumbling allowed.

But let's say, the children are invited. Guest
duties abound.

1. Respond to the invitation in a timely manner.
   (Formal wedding invitations require a written
   response.) R.s.v.p. is mandatory, not optional.
   R.s.v.p. and "Regrets Only" are not the same
   thing.

2. Dress appropriately for the occasion. Children should not wear the same thing to a wedding that they wear to play. Dressing up also establishes that the occasion is special and signals an expectation of proper behavior.

3. Use the occasion as a teaching opportunity so children know there are heightened expectations at such occasions. Talk about how we honor the couple with our presence. Explain the importance of the wedding and its solemn and serious meaning. Praise them when they respond appropriately.

4. Avoid the *"Hope they'll be okay—they didn't take a nap today"* wishful thinking approach to taking toddlers and infants into a special service. Most weddings today are recorded and crying infants and rambunctious toddlers will detract from the

R.s.v.p. is a French abbreviation for *"Respond, please."*

ceremony, get captured on a memorial
video, and cause guests dismay.

5. Take the children to the rest room before
    entering the ceremony.

6. Request a seat in the back or near an exit, so
    that you can slip out if necessary.

7. Caution children that just a whisper is
    allowed. The old saying, *"Children should be
    seen and not heard"* has a modern, welcome
    application to such special ceremonies.

8. Remember it's the Bride's day, and she gets
    to say who comes! Abide by her wishes;
    after all, it's her day!

"Pretty is as pretty does"

That's what grandmothers always say.

SOUTHERNERS GROW UP HEARING and, then when they're grown, saying *"Pretty is as pretty does."* There's a lot of truth in that well-worn saying.

Teaching our children to maintain an appropriate sense of decorum in public places would improve the lot of the world.

Here are the things to emphasize as some good manners in the public arena. Teach your child to:

1. Hold a door open for others and let others, especially adults, enter first.

2. Step aside after entering a doorway so that others coming after you are not blocked.

3. Stand back and kindly gesture that adults may precede you into an elevator.

4. Walk to the right in hallways and through airport concourses.

5. Whisper, if a brief conversation is necessary, in movie theatres, during cultural performances, at

weddings or at funerals—but issuing a loud
"Shhh—" is rude.

6. Walk in public buildings. Running is for the
   playground, ball field, or track.

7. Be conscientious of others when using a
   revolving door.

8. Remove a ball cap when indoors—especially
   in restaurants, auditoriums, churches.

9. Dispose of chewing gum properly. Wrap the
   used gum in paper before discarding.

10. Touch only the food you are going to eat
    while moving down a buffet line. If you touch
    it, it's yours!

11. Take your place in line and resist the urge to
    move up before your turn. Saving places for
    lots of friends is disrespectful to those waiting
    patiently for their turns.

12. Be punctual. Arrive on time for engagements.
    Better a little early than a little late!

Going visiting has its own set of rules.

The homes where children live are their training grounds. That's where they are taught right from wrong, kindness from unkindness, courtesy from discourtesy. And it's when they venture out of that setting that their manners are put on public display.

We must teach our children to display special consideration for others' homes and the rules established by the family that resides there.

We want our children to be welcome guests, and so we should caution them about these discourtesies:

- Coming unannounced into a home, whether the door is open or not (Knocking to signal our presence is a courtesy.)

- Neglecting to greet the family members who are at home

- Opening closets and cabinet doors or looking into drawers which should be off-limits

- Asking for food

- Helping ourselves to drinks in the refrigerator or cake on the counter, without being invited

- Squealing and running

- Using the telephone without permission

- Roaming into the private areas of another's home, such as into a master bedroom or a home office (It is inconsiderate because it presumes a privilege before it is granted.)

- Leaving without picking up behind ourselves, whether it's a glass, napkin, or toy

For a quick lesson in proper cap etiquette, encourage your children to observe the courteous way in which Tiger Woods removes his cap to show respect to other golfers, acknowledge the gallery, or accept his many trophies.

• Departing without saying goodbye and thanking our hosts for opening their home.

Young children should also be taught that they are not to ask to take things that belong to others home with them.

Southern children are often admonished, *"Now, don't be ugly!"* That is often a "send-off" remark, reminding our children that we have behavior standards and we expect these standards to be met. And that admonition most certainly applies when our children are in other people's homes and not under their parent's watchful eye.

Pouting falls under the *"Now, don't be ugly"* category. Southerners will often chide their children with this remark, *"Don't stick out your lip, you're liable to step on it!"*

"Mr. David"
AND
"Miss Susan"

. . . and other forms of address

RECENTLY I HAD A LADY (Southerners respectfully refer to the female gender as lady, rather than woman) ask me why her daughter-in-law of several years would continue, even after the wedding, to refer to her husband and her with the formal use of Mr. and Mrs. She felt first name references were in order as parents of the husband. I was called upon to explain.

~

In the South, the use of honorifics is considered a sign of respect and is widely observed across generations. My mother called my daddy's mother by a formal title until the day my grandmother died at the age of 97. My husband stills refers to my mother with a formal title. It is a formality taught in Southern homes.

To Southern sensibilities, it would be improper to presume the familiarity of an elder by the use of a first name.

definition of honorific

A complimentary title used to address a person and to denote respect or to confer honor. Everyone is entitled to an honorific (some are just fancier than others): Mr., Mrs., Ms., Dr., Judge, Mayor

Even after this particular couple had requested that their daughter-in-law revert to calling them by their first names, the formality had continued. They were baffled, but I explained it was a tenet of her upbringing. A first name basis is usually established only when both parties are willing.

An honorific combined with a first name (*"Miss Anne"*) is used for very close friends of the family. This less formal address, granted with double permission from the special friends and the child's parent, signals a unique relationship. Neighbors for many decades or best friends of the child's parents are two instances where this special circumstance may exist.

"You were so kind"

A N D

other writing courtesies

Dear "Wow,"
You gave me
nine wonderful dollars
for my ninth birthday.
Now I can buy
a new drawing pad
and pencils. My first
picture will be for you.
Love,
Alaina

"Wow" is Alaina's grandmother.

WHEN THE BOLINGS, our next door neighbors of many years, retired and moved away, Mrs. Boling gave me a parting gift that I'll never forget. She returned to me all the thank you notes that our two sons had written her over the years. Some were little notes for her delicious chocolate chip cookies; some for birthday gifts, others for graduation gifts. It was a treasure trove of nostalgia, a gift I won't soon forget, and a reminder that teaching our children to write notes may have unexpected, delightful consequences!

Stationery should be fun, pens should be colorful and stamps should be interesting! We have to do everything we can to entice our children to grow into the habit of writing notes—and not only thank you notes. Notes are also appropriate for any gesture of kindness— to a neighbor who fed your dog while you were away, to your friend's grandmother who invited you over for watermelon, or to a store clerk who located your misplaced jacket.

words often misspelled or misused during note writing

Congratulations	no "d"—a "t" instead
Sincerely	2 e's
Yours truly	no apostrophe in Yours; truly has no e and is not capitalized
Your	possessive of you
You're	contraction for You are
Ninety	includes an e
It's	contraction for It is
Its	no apostrophe—possessive form of it
There	not here, but over there
Their	belonging to them—possessive form
They're	contraction for They are
Lovely	includes an e
Precious	includes an i
Special	(seven letters: it's just a difficult word for children to spell)

A well-written note may be short in length, but it should possess several characteristics. It should be:

- neat, crisp, and clean. (no smudges, bent or torn corners, spots, erasure holes, white-outs, or mark-throughs)

- correct in form and grammar. (margins on each side, a formal greeting including the salutation Dear, a couple or more sentences to form the body, a formal closing, a signature; close attention to punctuation, spelling, and sentence structure)

- thoughtful, honest, and worthy to be read.

A greeting in a note should begin with Dear followed by the name and then a comma. The first and last names are never used together—one or the other is correct. Dear Abigail, or Dear Mr. Spence, (*not* Dear Mr. Ed Spence) If a child has been granted permission and the child calls the recipient by an honorific and first name, the greeting may read Dear Miss Becky,

An effective note:

- focuses on the person to whom it is written, rather than primarily on the writer (does not begin the note with "I")

- provides an illustration, example, or detail to interest the reader and make the note special (tells a story or relates an incident that applies)

- selects interesting adjectives instead of tired, overused ones (great becomes remarkable; cute becomes wonderful)

- uses alliteration (repetition of consonant sounds at the beginning of words) when possible to add rhythm to the writing (wonderful wagon, perfect puzzle) which can be taught like a game

A thank you note should be more about the gift

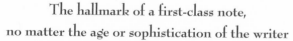

**The hallmark of a first-class note,
no matter the age or sophistication of the writer**
It's one the recipient wants to keep or share!

or the giver than the person who is writing the note.

An easy way to assure this perspective is to teach your children to begin the note with "You" or "Your," rather than "I."

"You sent me the best . . . .," or "Your gift really thrilled me . . ." rather than the more perfunctory "I want to thank you for the . . . ."

A little exercise in ensuring the note's message is tilted in the right direction is to teach your child to count the number of times the note contains personal pronoun references to the recipient (your, you) and to the writer (me, mine, my, I). The reference words to the recipient should exceed (or at least match) the number of references to the writer.

Create a handy list of appropriate adjectives for children who are learning to write thank you notes. Help them choose fancier words (instead of the worn-out, over-used adjectives "nice" and "great") as they grow in their writing skills.

fabulous	wonderful	enjoyable
exciting	fantastic	marvelous
amazing	delightful	special

Choice of adjectives should evolve as children grow in maturity.

Adjectives such as cute, cool, nice, and great are commonly used by beginning writers. As writers become more adept, their adjective list should expand and involve more descriptive words

Tucker's handprint and little scribbles

like wonderful, fabulous, and delightful.

And as Southern children grow in their Southern ways, they'll choose to describe things as precious, lovely, and darlin'— without the g! And *"interesting"* and *"unbelievable"* are some-times handy to describe gifts that defy describing!

Birthday gifts, Christmas gifts (and especially if it's money from grandparents) and overnight visits or other special hospitality rate written thank you notes!

Here's a good strategy. Tell your children they cannot play with the gift until the note is written!

"Don't you dare ..."
at the dinner table

GROWING UP IN THE SOUTH, we're often admonished, *"Don't you dare . . ."*

Here's a beginning list of things that children should be taught as they learn to dine with others. There are many more, but these are basic skills and a good place to begin.

"Don't you dare . . . begin eating as soon as a plate of food appears, with disregard for others sharing the meal. In formal meal settings, children should be taught to wait until the host or hostess (or parent) signals that the meal has begun. There may be a blessing that comes first, before anyone sips a beverage or lifts a piece of silverware.

"Don't you dare . . . chew with the mouth open. The perpetrators of this discourtesy may not realize how unpleasant it is for their dinner partners—and that certainly includes family members.

"*Don't you dare* . . . announce to a host that you don't like a particular food or the way it is prepared. "*Turning your nose up*" at food placed before you appears unkind and is discourteous.

"*Don't you dare* . . . speak loudly or harshly to your dining companions or those seated nearby.

"*Don't you dare* . . . beg food from others. "*Can I have a sip of your tea? Can I have your brownie if you aren't going to eat it?*" We each have portions that are our own. Even the more grammatically correct "*May I have a sip of your sweet tea?*" won't work to make this practice acceptable.

"*Don't you dare* . . . pierce a large portion of food and then eat several bites of it while it is still on the fork. Food should be cut up into bite size pieces.

"*Don't you dare* . . . eat from another person's plate. A person may offer to share a portion of his or her food with you, but it should be passed.

"Don't you dare . . . blow your nose at the table.
The napkin can be used for unexpected sneezes, or
even for a sniffle or two, but the diner who must
blow his nose should leave the table in consideration
to his dining companions. (This is good information
for grown-ups, too.)

"Don't you dare . . . expect to leave the table after
hurriedly eating. Children should be taught to sit
at the table until everyone is finished. (My niece

carries a "Busy Box" when she takes her little three-year-old daughter to a restaurant.)

"Don't you dare . . . withdraw from the table without first asking permission to be excused. *"May I be excused, please?"* is the proper phrasing, rather than *"Can I be excused?"* (If you wish to leave the table to go to the bathroom, your parents should know where you are going, but it is not necessary to announce to everyone at the table *"I need to go to the bathroom."* If you must leave the table, be sure it's for a very brief time out of consideration for the other guests at the table.)

Teach your children the difference between May and Can

May is the correct verb to use when asking permission—*"May I have another glass of lemonade, please?"* Can signals the ability to do something—*"I can write my name in cursive." "I can do that report on my computer."*

Teach your children to set a correct table: fork to the left, knife to the right, spoon to the right. The sharp edge of the knife blade should be next to the plate.

Helpful hint: Fork has four letters and a fork is found to the left of the plate. Left also has four letters. Knife and spoon both have five letters. Both are found to the right of the plate. Right also has five letters.

At a correct table setting, the fork is not correctly placed on top of the napkin, but rather to the left side of the plate. The napkin may be placed to the left of the fork(s) or on top of the plate. The napkin would be the first thing lifted from the table so it should not have anything on top of it, which would have to be picked up and moved.

It's no small thing to learn to handle utensils well, and the best time to learn is very young.

The first place to start is with correctly sized utensils. To expect a five-year-old to handle a regular adult-sized dinner fork (or even the adult-sized salad fork) is akin to asking an adult to eat his meal with the cold meat fork—a rather large serving piece.

Children should move through four levels of silverware, as they learn to eat.

First is the infant feeding spoon, a long, narrow

tapered utensil with a small oval-shaped bowl.

Second is the toddler pair of utensils, a small fork and its matching small spoon, approximately four inches in length. The tines of the fork are broad and short; the bowl of the spoon is rather large in proportion to its length.

Third is the most neglected of the group, the youth set*. It contains a trio of pieces, matching knife, fork, and spoon. The distinguishing characteristic of this vital set is that it is a miniature replica of the traditional adult size, but it is shaped and fashioned for the smaller hands of children.

Sizes vary according to pattern, but most youth sets are between one and two inches shorter than their adult counterparts. In my sterling pattern, the youth fork is 5-1/2 inches in length, the fork is 6-1/4 inches in length, and the youth knife is 7

*For ordering information, see the copyright page.

inches in length. They are also lighter, and thus easier for smaller hands to handle.

Fourth, of course, is the customary adult set which their parents would use on a daily basis.

Holding the fork and knife correctly is the single most important dining skill that children should be taught. Grasping a fork like a dagger or a holding a knife with the fist may allow some leverage, but it is improper and should be corrected each time it appears. (And it will continue to appear repeatedly unless you are diligent and consistent in your teaching!) Learning on utensils that are properly scaled to hand size simplifies the lesson immensely.

When the dinner fork is used to convey food to the mouth, it rests firmly on the middle finger, with the index finger and the thumb above the handle of the fork to steady it. Children should be taught that three fingers are below the handle and two fingers above. (Often children hold a pencil with this grasp.)

It gets trickier when the fork and knife are turned downward to cut a piece of food. Whether left-handed or right-handed, the diner should hold the fork in the left hand, turned with the tines down, and the knife in the right hand, turned with the blade down. The index finger should point to

the downward tines and the remaining four fingers curl around the handle of the fork. The same position is correct for the knife. The index finger points toward the end of the blade, and the remaining four fingers curl around the knife handle.

Two things apply for the correct handling of both utensils: the index finger points and the index finger should not share space on the upper handle with any of the other fingers.

In this one instance, it is quite all right to teach your children to point!

When you have finished your meal and are ready for the wait staff to remove your plate, position your fork and knife at 4:00 on the plate, as if the plate was the face of a clock. The fork is positioned below the knife. Their handles may extend about an inch off the plate. This placement signals to the wait staff that you are finished with your meal and are ready for your plate to be removed. Waiters remove your plate from the right.

There's plenty more to learn, but these are important first skills.

BEING RAISED SOUTHERN is really a privilege. It's more than just growing up in a certain locale, or being taught to say *"No, Ma'am"* and *"Yes, Sir."* It's a glorious way to honor people and spread kindness—and it's taught by parents and grandparents alike who want to inspire these virtues in their children. Bless your hearts, teach them well—not only for their benefit but for us all.